A Message from Sam Poynter and Emma Rorke, founders of Chic and Cheerful charity boutique

'A good head and a good heart are always a formidable combination.'
Nelson Mandela

We remember vividly the day Molly rang us to tell us about her vision of *Molly's Style Icons*. The excitement in her voice was palpable as she rang each of us and hurriedly got her words out to explain her ideas and some of the responses she had received. It was clear at that moment that her school project had legs and was going to become something great.

Molly encapsulates what it is to be a child, full of joy, enthusiasm and a 'think can' attitude. She is full of creative flair and her entrepreneurial spirit is evident in this wonderful idea for her book.

Molly's capacity to connect and understand the injustice of poverty – that children can go hungry or cannot go to school simply by virtue of where they were born – has always touched us deeply. Ever since that day on the sofa when she was just seven, she has always been finding ways to help raise funds for the children who live thousands of miles away from her and whom she will probably never meet.

As the quote from Nelson Mandela says, a good head and good heart are a formidable combination and we feel that Molly is a living example of this.

We are so appreciative of her great efforts to assist the children and families that Chic and Cheerful fundraises for and wish her the very best in her first publication. Go Molly! You are great!

Love Sam Poynter and Emma Rorke xx

Molly's Style Icons

MOLLY PARMETER is twelve years old and a first year student in Kilkenny College. Molly lives in Athy, County Kildare, with her parents and her brother, Jim.

One of Molly's main interests is the performing arts. She enjoys ballet and modern dance. She has performed in many ballet shows in the George Bernard Shaw Theatre in Carlow and recently played the role of the 'bold mouse' in *The Tales of Beatrix Potter*.

Since the age of four, Molly has been a member of Spotlight Stage School, under producer Stuart O'Connor. She performed in the opening of *The Late Late Toy Show* (2010), the *Eurovision Winner's Show* in the Bord Gáis Energy Theatre (2012) and Jedward' s Carlow concert (2012) as a hip-hop dancer. She was chosen to perform in the Olympia panto, *Jedward and the Magic Lamp* (2012-13), in which she did a run of seventeen shows. Molly also sang in the children's chorus in Opera Theatre Company's performance of *Carmen* in the George Bernard Shaw Theatre in 2013.

Molly attends weekly art classes and has won many art competitions locally and in her school. Her poster entry won the senior Benson Memorial Prize, 2013, in the art competition for the schools of the Diocese of Cashel, Ossory and Ferns. Molly also enjoys playing cricket with Carlow Cricket Club.

Molly's Style Icons

Molly Parmeter

First published in 2013
by Londubh Books
18 Casimir Avenue, Harold's Cross, Dublin 6w, Ireland
www.londubh.ie

1 3 5 4 2

Cover illustrations by Molly Parmeter
Cover design by bluett
Layout by David Parfrey; set in Aleo and Adobe Garamond Pro
Printed by Gráficas Castuera, Navarra, Spain

ISBN: 978-1-907535-33-8

Women think of all colours except the absence of colour.
I have said that black has it all. White too.
Their beauty is absolute. It is the perfect harmony.

Coco Chanel

for Jim, Jo-Jo and Ben…
three great men

Contents

Foreword by Lorraine Keane

What fun to be involved with Molly's book. It ticks all the boxes for me. The first is working with women: Molly, the compiler of the book, and Sam and Emma, the founders of Chic and Cheerful charity boutique in Carlow. Women are some of the most important people in my life – my daughters, my mum, my five sisters, my granny (ninety-three this year); friends I have had since school; girlfriends I have had the good fortune to meet throughout my studies and career; my mother-in-law and sisters-in-law. Without these women in my life it would be a very dull place and, honestly, I don't think I could have progressed or achieved success without their love and support.

I am lucky enough to work with two of my sisters in my professional career: Tori is a hair stylist and Becky a make-up artist. I always remind my two girls (Emelia, nine, and Romy, six) how important sisters are in your life. I can't believe that Molly is only two years older than Emelia. It does my heart good to see such talent and imagination in a young lady like Molly.

Chic and Cheerful supports a kindergarten in Ethiopia, feeding three hundred and ninety children a day in that country, as well as helping one hundred and seventy children in Kenya to go back to school. Food, water and education – basic rights that we take for granted – give these children hope for the future. It *gives* them a future.

It is no secret that I have a passion for clothes and fashion of all kinds. I love Irish designers and really believe they're as good as any of the international designers so I'm delighted that some of them feature in this book. I also love high street and mixing it with more investment pieces. I think that's the key to an individual look that's full of personality. I hope that's why Molly chose me as one of her style icons for the book: I was so flattered when her letter arrived.

I know from writing my own book a couple of years ago how much work is involved in a project like this: writing the text, choosing the illustrations and so on. Molly sent out letters to all her chosen style icons – and reminder letters to a good few of them, judging by some of the replies reproduced here – and did a lovely, atmospheric drawing of each of the style items they nominated. Her book contains fifty-four of these drawings. Then she had to find a publisher who was willing to devote the time and energy and funds to producing it and putting it in the shops (another woman, Jo O'Donoghue of Londubh Books). Finally, Molly's dream is about to come to fruition and book-buyers, people-watchers and fashionistas of Ireland will have a lovely gift item for Christmas 2013, whether for themselves, their friends, their clients or their customers.

Well done Molly! You are a credit to your school, your family and your home county of Kildare. I hope *Molly's Style Icons* raises lots of money for Chic and Cheerful projects in Ethiopia and Kenya. Every year I travel to the world's poorest countries on behalf of Trócaire and World Vision, to highlight the incredible work they do, and it's the saddest thing you ever saw. Children there do not know where their next meal is coming from or whether they will even make it to their fifth birthday. These are harsh realities for millions of people, realities that might not exist if there were more Molly Parmeters in the world.

Next time I'm in Carlow I'll certainly be paying a visit to Chic and Cheerful boutique, looking for that once-in-a-lifetime vintage find and knowing that, at the same time, I will be helping to support the charity's important work.

Molly's Style Icons brings together some of the great interests and passions of my life so it is a pleasure and a privilege for me to write the foreword. Thank you, Molly, for choosing me as one of your style icons in the first place and for asking me to write the foreword.

I really look forward to seeing the book.

Lorraine Keane
August 2013

Introduction

I remember the day my mum brought me into Chic and Cheerful for the first time. We walked into the shop and I saw it was full of treasures. My mum had explained to me that she was going to volunteer there from now on.

I loved it from the minute I stepped over the threshold. 'Chic' and 'cheerful' were the two best words to describe it. My mum introduced me to Sam, one of the founders of the charity. Sam led me over to a comfy couch and took out a photo album. She told me about the work the charity did and went through the album. It was full of pictures of smiling boys and girls my age and even younger. Then Sam showed me photos of the dirty streets and homes where these children had lived and told me how she and Emma, the other founder of Chic and Cheerful, and all the volunteers helped these hungry children.

As I grew older, I became more interested in art and fashion. I loved finding old scarves and broken jewellery in the shop and making things with them. I couldn't believe what lovely bits and bobs people so kindly donated. It was such a joy to decorate the shop window with these beautiful things. For Christmas my brother would buy me a *Vogue* magazine and for my ninth birthday I got tickets to the Elaine Curtis Fashion Show in Carlow. I really enjoyed it and was very impressed that the proceeds went to local charities. That's how I decided to do a style bible, using my passion for art and fashion to help other children.

Sam and Emma have inspired me so much. I am grateful to them both for their example and encouragement. I would like to thank all the style icons who kindly responded to my letter asking them to open their wardrobe and tell me about their favourite item. I hope my drawings do justice to their special replies. Finally I want to thank Frank Standish, without whose kind assistance the publication of this book would not have been possible.

I hope you enjoy the book.

Love
Molly

Molly's Invitation to Style Icons

Dear Style Icon

My name is Molly Parmeter. I am eleven years old and am a sixth-class pupil in Carlow National School. I live with my parents and my nine-year-old brother in Athy, County Kildare. I enjoy dancing, both modern and ballet, and attend the local stage school and choir. I have a huge interest in fashion and art and am lucky enough to attend Iwona Nartowska-O'Reilly for weekly art lessons.

Every year as part of my schoolwork I do a project. This year I would like to do a style bible type of book where I would write to stylish people just like you and find out what you and other style icons think is the most stylish item of clothing you can have in your wardrobe! I will then illustrate this item of clothing.

Along with fulfilling my school work requirements I could try and sell this book with the proceeds going to a local Carlow charity shop, Chic and Cheerful boutique, where my mum volunteers and where I also help out doing themed window displays (www.chicandcheerful.ie). This is a charity that supports orphan children in Ethiopia and Kenya. It is a really fabulous charity and is completely volunteer led. This shop feeds 390 children a day in Ethiopia and supports 200 children through their education in Kenya.

As money is short now with everyone in Ireland the shop needs to think of different ways to fundraise and I thought this might be a good one. I would be so grateful if you could take the time to drop me a quick line to tell me what you think is the most stylish item you can have in your wardrobe. I will attempt to illustrate this very nicely and if it all works out I will send you your very own copy!

Thank you so, so much.

Kind regards
Molly

Rachel Allen

Chef and Food Writer, Ballymaloe, County Cork

Dear Molly

Thank you for your lovely letter. You certainly have a busy life. I loved art and fashion when I was growing up too.

My choice for the most stylish item has to be a fitted black jacket. You can put it over a dress in the evening time or you can dress up a pair of jeans to look smart. It's a very versatile piece of clothing and everyone should have one in their wardrobe.

I hope this is of help, I look forward to seeing your style bible.

Kind regards
Rachel Allen

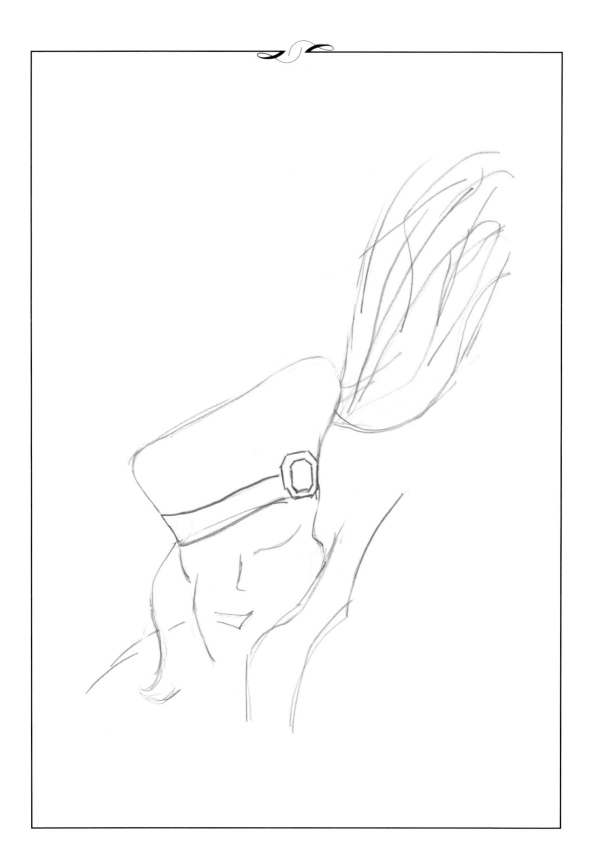

Faith Amond

Stylist and Milliner, County Carlow

Molly

Firstly I apologise sincerely for delay in replying.

I enclose a photograph which appeared in *VIP Magazine* in 2011.

My suit is from Touch of Class Boutique, Carlow, and my headpiece is certainly one of my favourites, a Philip Treacy.

I wish you every success with your project, the style bible.

Love
Faith

Catriona Ashmore

Fashionista, Elaine Curtis, Carlow

Dear Molly

Apologies for taking so long to reply but unfortunately I have been unwell. I was delighted and very flattered to get your lovely letter and what a great idea you have to create a style bible!

To answer your question, I think the most stylish item to have in your wardrobe is a pair of HIGH HEELS! They are a must for any fashion-savvy girl. They must be black (leather or patent), no platform sole, nice slim heel and pointed toe…even better if they have the covetable red sole (Christian Louboutin). This style of shoe can take the wearer effortlessly from day to night; these shoes also look great with everything: jeans, dresses, skirts and trousers! They are the best investment any girl will ever make.

To me personally, I think good shoes are the basis of an outfit. Clothes can be cheaper but with great shoes the overall look can change. Also, from a female perspective, it doesn't matter what size waist you have, your shoes will always fit!

My favourite shoes – I saved for a long time before making the investment – are black patent Christian Louboutin 100 heels, so high I feel nearly six foot tall in them. They cost a lot on the day I bought them but from the amount of wear I get from them, they don't owe me a penny!

I wish you all the best in your project and I hope I am not too late with this reply. Enjoy making your book…you may well be the first Irish/Australian editor of British *Vogue*.

Catriona x

Zeta Ashmore

Budding Style Icon (aged ten), County Carlow

Hello Molly

My favourite item from my mum's wardrobe is a pair of Miu Miu sparkly gold, peep-toe, high-heeled shoes with a black velvet bow.

Zeta

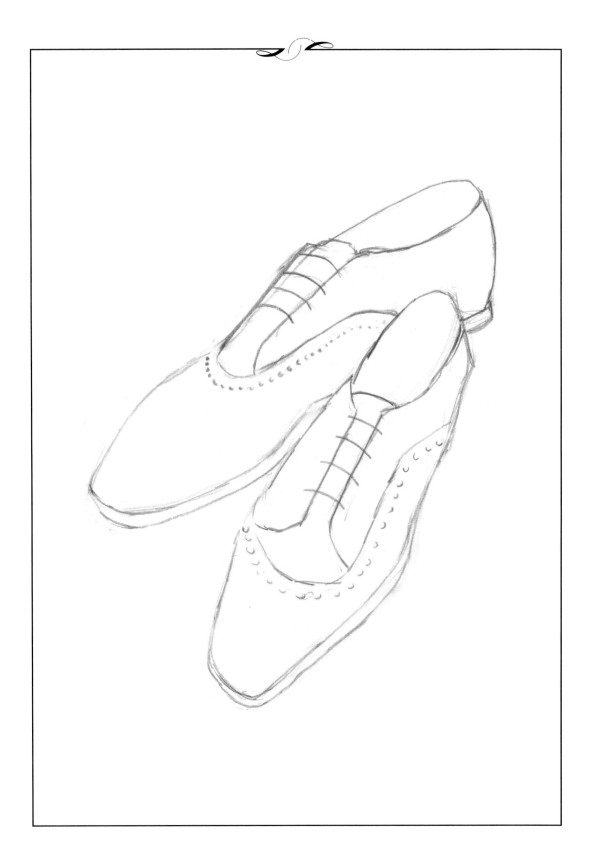

J.S. Bolger

Horse Trainer, County Carlow

Dear Molly

Being a trainer of race horses I regularly hear the idiom, 'No foot no horse'. How true it is and whoever coined it hit the nail on the head.

After my mind, the part of my body which gets the most use is my feet. It follows that I should take good care of them. I use them almost all day long and I could not envisage a time when I could do my job without them. Therefore I always try to have a few good pairs of well-made boots and shoes.

As I am a foreign currency earner through training horses for international groups and exporting Irish horses to Australia, Dubai, China, Eastern Europe and the USA, I don't feel unpatriotic in purchasing boots and shoes from Italy.

Therefore if I exhibit any style at all one has to look south to see. They can be black or brown. According to an old acquaintance, brown must not be worn after seven and never in the city! So if I am seen scurrying home of a late evening I must be wearing brown shoes!

Gravati and Artioli make my boots and Jackie (my long suffering wife) very kindly gave me a pair of handmade Artioli shoes in black, which should see me out, showing no sign of wear after five years.

I hope you raise buckets of money for needy children and I congratulate you on your caring disposition.

Yours sincerely
J.S. Bolger

Joan Burton TD

Minister for Social Protection

Dear Molly

Thank you so much for your letter and asking me to participate in your style bible project. As a woman politician, one of the stylish items I like to have in my wardrobe is a light-coloured jacket – white or pink are among my favourites. I find these colours look very cheerful, especially if the day is dull.

I have included with this letter an example of a recent photo where I am wearing a light pink jacket and red shoes.

You sound like you are a very lucky girl with a lot of interesting hobbies, including dancing, fashion and art.

I wish you all the best with the new school term and hope that your style bible project helps raise lots of money for the local charity where your mum volunteers.

Kind regards
Joan Burton TD
Minister for Social Protection

Gabriel Byrne

Actor, New York

Dear Molly

Thank you for your letter. Your idea to help Chic and Cheerful is a terrific one.

The item I would choose is a double-breasted cashmere overcoat in black.

I hope this will be helpful to you for your drawing.

I also enclose a donation to put towards your fund.

Very best regards
Gabriel Byrne

Gay Byrne

Broadcaster, Dublin

Dear Molly

My most stylish item is a lovely black leather jacket I bought in John Taylor's shop in Baggot Street, Dublin.

Lined, cosy and warm!

I wish you luck with your project.

Gay Byrne

Jean Byrne

Meteorologist, Dublin

Dear Molly

Many thanks for your letter and invitation to participate in your style bible. It sounds like a great idea and the charity is a very worthwhile cause so I hope you raise loads of funds!

Difficult to say exactly what could be the most stylish item in one's wardrobe! If I were allowed just one item, I would choose a simple black dress, (or another neutral shade, depending on one's complexion), but one which is beautifully cut/tailored, with the finest cloth. This is because it can be so versatile. I can dress it 'up' for a night out, with jewellery and other accessories such as crystal collars, fur or faux fur. It can be worn to work or to a business meeting in an understated way, with nice heels and handbag, and the look can be changed yet again, by using an interesting belt or sash/obi around the waist.

If I could be allowed another stylish item, it would be a hat. I regard these as works of art, as sculptures, and they can transform any outfit in a unique and very stylish way!

I hope that these thoughts are of some help to you.

Wishing you the very best with your venture.

Jean Byrne

Catherine, Duchess of Cambridge

St James's Palace, London

Dear Molly

The Duchess of Cambridge has asked me to thank you for the lovely letter you recently sent in which you wrote so enthusiastically about your school project in which you intend to produce a style bible.

Her Royal Highness receives many letters and unfortunately this means she is unable to respond personally to each one. However, I can say on her behalf that the Duchess does not have a single item of clothing that she would consider to be the most stylish of her clothes. I apologise for the disappointment that this may cause you but nevertheless, I do hope that you are able to complete your project.

The Duchess of Cambridge was immensely touched that you should take time to write to her as you did. It really was most thoughtful of you and Her Royal Highness has asked me to send you her warmest thanks and best wishes.

Yours sincerely
Mrs Claudia Holloway

Marie Chawke

Hotel and Spa Manager, Aghadoe Heights Hotel, Killarney, County Kerry

Dear Molly

Thank you for your lovely letter and well done on this project. It sounds like you are doing wonderful work for Chic and Cheerful.

One of my favourite items of clothing in my wardrobe is my cashmere Louise Kennedy wrap, which I cherish and mind so carefully. This was a gift I received and I must admit it is one of the most beautiful garments I possess, from the sumptuous delicate cashmere nude-beige fabric to the subtle detailing. I just love to wear this wrap.

It is so versatile, ideal for travelling and the perfect accessory to finish off any outfit, whether it is for casual or formal wear. Like all Louise's designs, it exudes style and stunning technique and is a testament to her exquisite attention to detail. True to Louise, my wrap has the Kennedy hallmarks – an insistence on impeccable finish and precious fabrics.

So as you can see, this is one of the favourite items of clothing, which I will treasure for a long time and continue to fold, store and wrap in tissue paper!

Molly, I hope your book is a huge triumph and I wish you continued success with your love for fashion and art.

Warmest regards
Yours sincerely
Marie Chawke

Derry Clarke

Restaurateur, L'Ecrivain, Dublin

Dear Molly

Thank you so very kindly for your lovely letter. What a wonderful project! I am very flattered and honoured that you contacted me to be a part of it.

My favourite item of clothing would have to be shirts! I wear them every day with either trousers or jeans. I have lots and lots of colourful shirts with cool patterns and designs. My favourite one has to be my purple-grey shirt with red and blue flowers on it.

My chef's uniform is white and I wear it a lot so when I'm not working, it's nice to wear colours! Colours are a great way to express yourself and I find that my clothes reflect my personality, very outgoing!

I wish you the very best of luck with your book and look forward to seeing your book on the shelves.

Warm regards
Derry Clarke

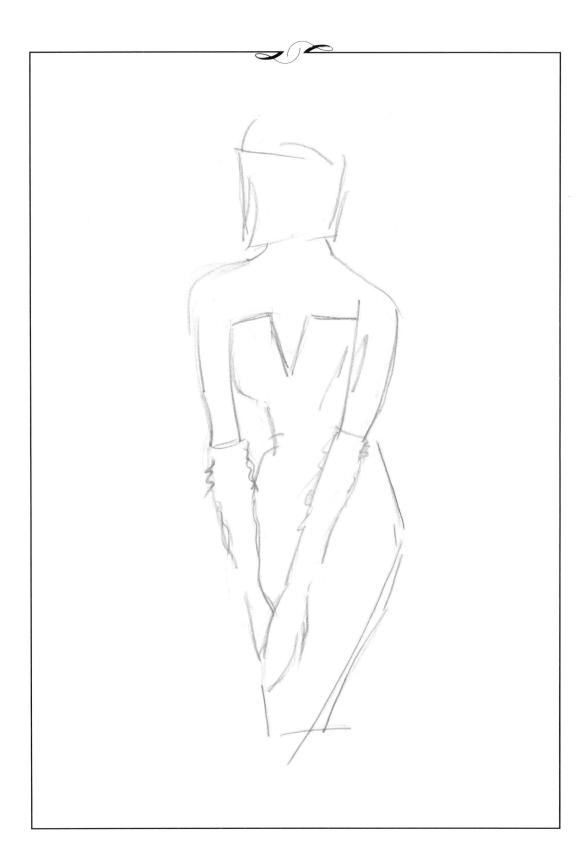

Martina Collins

Satina Boutique, Tramore, County Waterford

Dear Molly

I am sorry for the delay in replying to your letter. I have been travelling a lot lately, preparing for the spring-summer 2013 season.

The LBD, little black dress, is the answer to every woman's dilemma when preparing for a special occasion.

I wish you every success with your style bible book and also raising money for the charity shop, Chic and Cheerful.

Again please accept my apology for the delay.

Yours sincerely
Martina Collins

Louis Copeland

Men's Retailer, Dublin

Hi Molly

Firstly, I think what you are doing is absolutely terrific and I wish you every success with it. And thank you for asking me to contribute! I hope what I have written below is OK. If anything doesn't 'suit', please feel free to come back to me.

I suppose in my business it is important to look a little bit different – it is, I suppose, almost expected! My favourite garment has to be my pinstripe suit. I like a pronounced stripe, usually on a navy wool cloth, and would normally team it with a colourful shirt and tie combination.

I tend to wear quite a lot of pink or blue shirts and strong colourful ties. I love it when people comment on (or slag!) my ties. In a social environment nothing gives me more pleasure than seeing someone wear a tie that is a talking point for all his friends – without being tacky, of course!

However, having said all that, day to day, the suit I probably wear more than any other is a plain navy suit. For men, the navy suit is really an equivalent of the ladies' 'little black dress'. It is suitable for every occasion and depending on where you are going, you can tone it down or dress it up. Almost every shirt and tie a man will find in his wardrobe will go with a navy suit.

Every bit as important for me, though, and the one accessory I never leave home without, is my measuring tape! I feel naked without it! You just never know when and where someone will need to be measured…

Kindest regards
Louis

Shelly Corkery

Fashion Director, Brown Thomas,
Grafton Street, Dublin

Dear Molly

Thank you so much for your lovely letter. I do hope I am not too late with my response. I have been travelling lots for the New York and London fashion weeks and will be moving on to Milan and Paris next. Working in fashion is hard work but great fun and I'm glad you take such an interest. It is also great to see that someone at your young age is involved in charity projects.

With regards to your project, I will gladly contribute. I have quite a few favourites in my wardrobe and it's so difficult to choose just one but I have to say my gold Christian Louboutin Pigalle shoes are fabulously stylish and a firm favourite! I have a few pairs of Louboutins but the Pigalles are just lovely. When I wear them I feel so dressed up and special, as they are pointed, elegant and feminine with lots of sparkles. I *love* feminine glamour, I *love* high heels and I *adore* sparkles!

Good luck with your project, Molly!

Kindest regards
Shelly

Brendan Courtney

Broadcaster/Fashion Designer

Dear Molly

What a wonderful idea for a great cause. You are fantastic.

The most stylish item in my wardrobe is my favourite three-piece vintage tweed jacket, trousers and waistcoat (suit).

It was made in 1972 (so it is the same age as me!). I bought it for just €70. Very happy boy!

Best of luck and lots of love
Brendan

Karen Crawford

Smock Boutique, Drury Street, Dublin

Dear Molly

I hope you are well. Thank you so much for your lovely letter and I really like your idea for your style bible. Chic and Cheerful is a wonderful shop and well done for helping your mum. You must be very creative because not everyone can imagine interesting window displays to catch people's eye. I have a nine-year-old daughter called Ruby and she comes to work some Saturday mornings with me and she draws pictures on the blackboard we have in the shop, telling people what is 'new in'. She is a lot better at art than me!

I am delighted to give you any information you need to get your style bible up and running, so feel free to ask any other questions. There are a few things personal to me that I feel are stylish and that I would have in my wardrobe…

- A black tuxedo jacket, fitted and well shaped, that goes over most things I own.
- Black ankle boots, not too high
- Red lipstick
- A pearl necklace
- A pencil skirt

There are many more items but these would be my top tips because they are classic and timeless and individually can be worn in many different ways. However I am also very happy in my PJs at home! I wish you lots of success with your fundraising and well done for taking the time to do something for others who need it.

Warmest regards
Karen Crawford

AZZEDINE
ALAIA S/S12

Nikki Creedon

Havana Boutique, Donnybrook, Dublin

Dear Molly

Congratulations on such a wonderful letter and well done on your input into what sounds like a highly worthwhile charity.

My favourite item of clothing in my wardrobe is a coat by Azzedine Alaia. It is black and made from a heavy felt fabric, which gives it an amazing shape. It stands out at the end but is extremely fitted on top and always gets admired.

Please call me if I can be of any additional help.

Nikki

Elaine Curtis

Elaine Curtis Boutique, Carlow

Dear Molly

Thank you for your lovely letter and for considering me to be a style icon! I would be delighted to help you. I don't know where you get the time to fit a project like this in with everything else you do. You are one busy lady. You know, I always wondered who did those fab windows in Chic and Cheerful… now it all makes sense. One day we might be lucky enough to get you to do our windows. I hope things are going well for you all there. It's important to have shops like this in our community.

I must tell you that I have lots of bits and bobs over the years that I think are stylish for one reason or another so this is no easy task for me! I was also thinking that I should narrow it down to something colourful so that it would be easier for you to illustrate.

So I have come up with the following dress from the great Irish designer, Tim Ryan. I love this dress for many different reasons. It's a fantastic dress and is so different from anything else I own. I love the colours, the fringing, the way it moves when you walk and especially when you dance! It's also extremely comfortable. I have worn it lots and it has been worn lots by my sisters and friends. It's great to have a special dress that gets worn to special events by special people, don't you think? This dress is special because it was hand-made and hand-knitted by Tim, who is a friend of mine. We went to college together; I was studying fashion and Tim sculpture.

I hope you like this dress as much as me, Molly! Best of luck with the project. I'm looking forward to seeing it!

Best wishes
Elaine

Gillian Daly

Piano Teacher, Carlow College of Music

Dear Molly

Firstly, I want to compliment you on such a wonderful idea. It is so admirable to see a young lady like yourself supporting such a good cause.

I am flattered that you would consider me for your style bible and I hope I have something stylish to offer!

I am a strong believer in being unique and adding your own personal touch to your wardrobe, rather than following trends. I love cheerful and delicate colours and flowing dresses!

My favourite piece of clothing is my handmade silk scarf from India. It was made in a town called Varanasi and took twenty-eight days to complete. It holds so many memories for me because I purchased it during my time there and I will treasure it forever.

India is a country bustling with vibrant colour and charm. Native women wear the most magnificent traditional saris. During my time there, I embraced this wonderful way of dressing. Since I've returned, I wear my colourful silk scarf as a reminder of the wonderful time I had there that summer and the brilliant vibrancy of India and its people.

Best of luck, Molly, with this wonderful project.

Gillian Daly

Marietta Doran

Stylist, Borris, County Carlow

Hi Molly

Very best of luck with your book!

In relation to my most stylish item, thirteen years ago whilst on a shopping trip in Dublin looking for an outfit to wear to my daughter Mia's christening, I stopped by Brown Thomas and discovered the most beautiful little black dress I'd ever seen. It was from Miu Miu's autumn-winter 2000 collection. I loved their quirky take on something so classic.

There is a lot of detail to fall in love with: a simple scarf collar, long silk sleeves with hand-beaded cuffs and hem and gentle smocking detail on the waist.

I was hooked until I saw the price tag, which was not within my budget, so regretfully I didn't purchase it that day. A few weeks later a friend spotted the dress on sale, selling for considerably less. I bought it and subsisted on beans and toast for a few weeks.

Today, the dress gives me the same feeling of glamour and style as it did on the day of Mia's christening – a testament to its quality and design.

I've held on to this dress because it's like an old photograph that brings back many memories and that's what makes it special.

Lots of best wishes
Marietta Doran

PS You are a lovely girl. Looking forward to reading the book.

Wendy Duggan

Head of Marketing and PR, A Wear, Dublin

Dear Molly

Firstly I would just like to thank you for your lovely letter. It is great to hear from a fellow fashionista.

The volunteer work you and your mum do for Chic and Cheerful sounds fantastic. It seems to have a huge impact on the children in Ethiopia and Kenya. I really hope this book you are working on succeeds. It's great to see that you are putting in a big effort at school also.

One thing to remember is that everyone has their own style and due to trends changing every season one piece of clothing which I feel works for both autumn and winter is a nice floral print wrap dress. It can be worn in the warmer months with just a light cardigan and a pair of flats or heels, depending, and then in the winter months with contrasting tights, layering scarves and a nice blazer.

I hope this gives you an insight into what you are looking for. Feel free to look up some of our clothing pieces on www.awear.com. You can see some of our autumn-winter looks on this site to give you some further ideas. I wish you all the best with your book and school. I hope it all goes well.

Thanks a million
Wendy Duggan

Kenny Egan

Boxer and Olympic Medallist, Dublin

Dear Molly

My favourite item of clothing is the denim jacket.

I have chosen it because it is different and I want to bring back the double denim look from the 1980s.

Kenny

Louise Flanagan

Kalu Boutique, Naas, County Kildare

Dear Molly

Thank you so much for including me in your style bible.

My most special piece is my Jemima Khan cream cashmere coat with sequin collar and sequins on the pockets. Only for special occasions as it is very glamorous and unique. (I can send you a pic from my phone if that would help.) Just ring the store with your mobile number.

Warm regards
Louise
xx

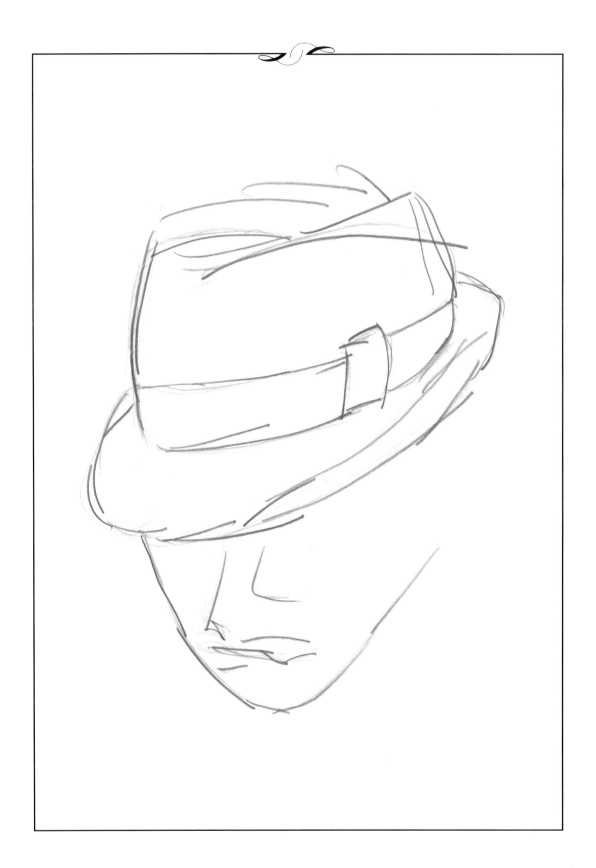

Michael Flatley

Dancer, County Cork

Dear Molly

Thank you for your letter which we received a few weeks ago.

Michael always loves receiving letters from fans. He is overseas so I scanned and forwarded your letter to him. He has come back to say that he considers a classic Borsalino hat to be the most stylish item in his wardrobe.

Can I just say that I think this is a fantastic project to be involved with. Not only are you getting the chance to develop your writing and drawing skills but you are helping others at the same time.

I hope you get great enjoyment and success out of your hard work.

Best wishes
Vivienne O'Grady
private secretary to Michael Flatley

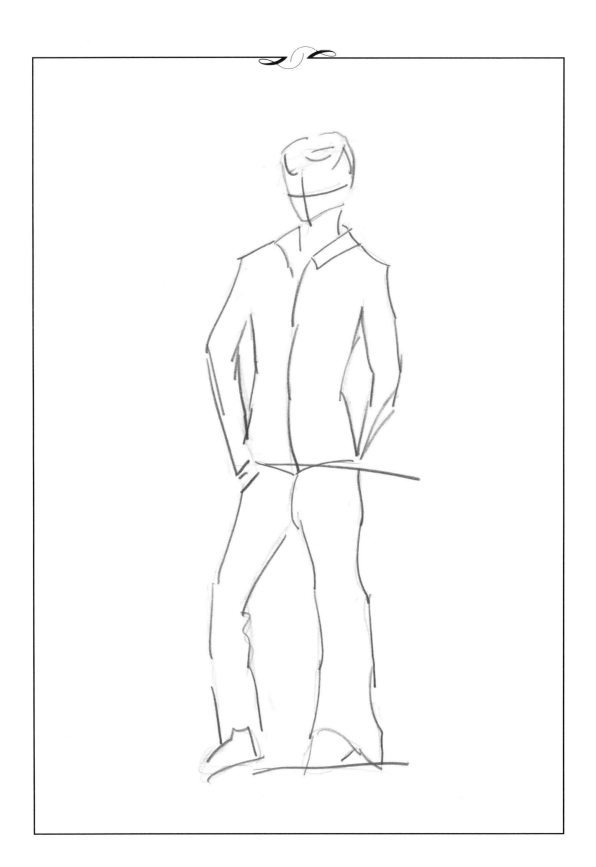

Sean Gallagher

Businessman, Dundalk, County Louth

Dear Molly

Thank you for your letter to Sean and well done on all your work with Love Shack.

Sean sends his apologies for not replying sooner. He was moving house and exceptionally busy.

Sean's favourite item of clothing is a suit with an open neck shirt (without a tie). He says this represents an entrepreneurial look and in it he is always readily dressed, no matter who he is meeting.

I hope this helps. Best of luck with the style bible.

Best wishes
Niamh
assistant to Sean Gallagher

P.J. Gibbons

Editor and Publisher, *Social and Personal* Magazine

Hi Molly

Sincere apologies for the delay in responding to you.

My favourite item of clothing would probably be a black blazer I've had for a few years. I think it's a Hackett jacket and I love it because it's so versatile that it can be worn to dress up or dress down and I generally wear it with jeans. I'm not really a suit person, so I like the fact that it can be both casual and dressy.

Is the above what you are looking for?

If you need anything else, just please email me back.

Many thanks and very best of luck with the book!

P.J.

Sarah Gill

Seagreen Boutique, Monkstown, County Dublin

Dear Molly

My sincere apologies for the delay in contacting you following your letter. We recently opened a second store in Ranelagh so I'm afraid I haven't been on top of the post here in Monkstown for the last couple of months.

My favourite piece in my wardrobe would have to be my J Brand 811 skinny jeans because they are so versatile. I can wear them with runners and a parka for a walk with my kids at the weekend or dress them up with heels and a pretty silk Equipment blouse for night-time.

Congratulations on a great idea and all the hard work that I am sure is going into it. I am looking forward to reading it when it comes out. I would love to be kept up to date on its progress.

Best regards
Sarah Gill

Mary Grant

Fashion Designer, Newbridge, County Kildare

Dear Molly

Many thanks for your lovely letter. You sound like a very busy young lady and I am impressed that you help your mum in Chic and Cheerful. That is a very worthwhile cause. Well done…you will probably run the country when you are older!

My favourite most stylish (or maybe not!) item in my wardrobe would have to be my black patent leather fourteen-hole Dr Martens. I have them about three years and I wear them at least three times every week. They go with everything I have in my wardrobe and even though they are cracked and have a hole in them now, I still love them.

My daughter who is sixteen has exactly the same ones and she has started wearing hers a lot. I was a bit disappointed about that as I thought perhaps I could pinch them – but no luck, I'm afraid. I'll just have to save up for a new pair!

I am sending you a few little things that maybe you can sell in the shop and a notebook for yourself that you can put all your ideas into.

Many thanks for including me in your project. I am very flattered!

Yours sincerely
Mary Grant

Mary Greene

Divine Boutique, Malahide, County Dublin, and Maynooth, County Kildare

Hi Molly

My apologies for the delay in responding to your letter but I had mislaid it and it went totally out of my head.

Many thanks for asking me to take part. I have had a really hard think about my 'favourite item', as I have too many and my most favourite item changes constantly!

At this moment I would have to say my most favourite item would be an electric-blue jumpsuit from my boutique, Divine. It is such a vibrant colour that whenever I wear it I get a real lift.

I am (and always was) a huge fan of jumpsuits (whether they are in fashion or not).

It is by a Danish designer, This Is Who I Am.

If you have any further queries, please do not hesitate to contact me.

Wishing you the very best of luck with your venture.

Kind regards
Mary

Heidi Higgins

Heidi Higgins Studio and Boutique,
Portlaoise, County Laois

Dear Molly

My apologies for such a late reply. I had misplaced your first letter but was thrilled to receive a reminder this morning!

My favourite item of clothing, without having to think about it too much, would have to be my 'Punchestown outfit', which it has now become known as! I wore a turquoise blue wool crèpe suit (jacket and dress with a printed chiffon polka-dot drape on the neckline, a design from my first collection) to my very first Ladies' Day a few weeks after I had launched my own studio and boutique in Portlaoise in April 2010.

It was my first day to leave my boutique in the hands of a friend who worked for me that day and it really was a great surprise to win Best Dressed Lady. I have lots of cherished memories from that day and my winning gave me great coverage in the press, which in turn gave me a fantastic start to my business. The turquoise wool crèpe suit with a silk trim is a classic Heidi Higgins design (luxurious fabric, simple cut with quirky detailing and bright bold colours)!

I have attached two images for you to see the outfit I am describing and I hope I have given you enough detail to help you get started on your book!

Wishing you lots of success with this very inspiring idea of yours!

Please do keep me posted. I would love to buy a copy.

Best wishes
Heidi

Celia Holman Lee

Stylist and Modelling Agent, Ballysheedy, County Limerick

Hi Molly

I hope I am not too late. I am coming off a very hectic season and I have not had a moment to sit down and go through all my email and letters, so apologies for the late correspondence.

What I consider to be my most stylish item is a dress! Whether it is for day or evening wear, a glamorous dress is my number one choice!

I also attach a picture to help your sketch! Let me know when your book is out. I would like to buy it!

Best of luck with it.

Kind regards
Celia Holman Lee

Gerald Kean

Solicitor, Dublin

Dear Molly

Just a short note to thank you for your lovely note. I wish you the best of luck with your project.

I will certainly contribute to a number of books when you are ready to put them on the market for sale!

You have chosen a great project.

My favourite item of clothing in the wardrobe is a Versace suit. I can send you photographs of the suit if necessary.

Please let me know how I can help.

Yours sincerely
Gerald Kean

Lorraine Keane

Broadcaster and Journalist

Dear Molly

I hope you had a nice Christmas and New Year. I am sure you are in bed now with school back tomorrow. The holidays go so fast, don't they?

Here is the photo of my favourite dress. I designed it with my friend Deborah Veale, a very famous Irish fashion designer. The editor of the magazine (*Irish Tatler*) told me that they were going to do the cover in red and gold so I contacted Deborah and told her I would like her to design the dress.

We bought the fabric together, I drew some ideas that I wanted and Deborah created this beautiful red silk dress. It had a big black bow around the waist that you cannot see in this picture. It was perfect for the Christmas cover. I borrowed the jewellery from my friend Annoushka, who is a jewellery designer.

I hope you like it!

All the best
Lorraine
x

Frank Lanigan

Solicitor, Carlow

Dear Molly

I'm an 'out-of-style' icon. My shoes are out of laces, shirts out of buttons, trousers out of zips, coats out of linings, toes out of socks, cufflinks out of order, colours out of fashion and I'm a constant embarrassment to my four daughters. I'd almost say that if you think I'm a style icon you would be 'out of' your mind.

That said, I have a little secret. My late uncle was a natty dresser, conservative but stylish. Once, when I was acting in a play, he lent me his favourite waistcoat and I never gave it back! There it is now in my wardrobe, a bright yellow, pure wool waistcoat with intricate mother of pearl buttons. Slightly tarnished and a little mothballed and that's just me!

But a style icon, nevertheless, at least in my little world. I haven't the nerve to wear it now but you'd never know.

Here's a little something for Chic and Cheerful.

Yours faithfully
Frank Lanigan

Sonya Lennon

Broadcaster/Fashion Designer, Dublin

Hi Molly

The most stylish item in my wardrobe is a 1960s Christian Dior *bombe* hat with a matching clutch. It is chocolate brown felt-trimmed, with three different-coloured snakeskin straps.

I bought it at a vintage fashion show. I ran backstage once the show was over so nobody else could buy it before me!

Hope this helps.

Kind regards
Sonya

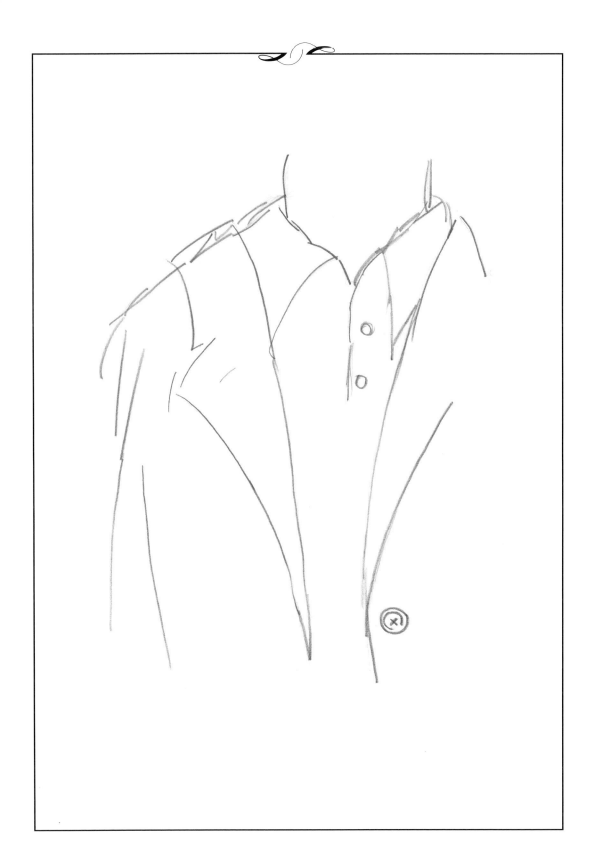

Dylan McGrath

Restaurateur, Rustic Stone, Dublin

Dear Molly

Thank you for your letter. I found the concept for your school project very exciting and would be delighted to help you in any way I can. It was great to hear of the work that you and you mum are doing in your local charity shop. Thinking of different ways of doing things isn't easy but you're right – as a result of people in Ireland having less money it is important that we do. I think your idea for another method of fundraising is very creative and innovative and in this environment, that's what it takes. There is no reason why this shouldn't be a great success.

I am flattered to be seen by some people as a 'style icon'. My brothers would disagree entirely but what would they know? To answer your question: I think the most stylish item of clothing I have in my wardrobe is a silver two-piece suit I bought for the IFTA [Irish Film and Television] awards one year. I bought it from a friend, Niall O'Farrell (from Dragons' Den), and he gave me a great deal on the suit as I was wearing it to the awards. So I would say that the most stylish item of clothing a man can have in his wardrobe is a suit – technically two items, I know, but if I had to pick, the blazer would win!

I hope this helps, Molly. You sound like a very interesting, hardworking and determined young lady and I wish you all success in the future. I have included a small voucher for you to use any time you like. If you are ever in Dublin with your family you should come and try some of the food in my restaurant. If you need anything else, please do not hesitate to contact me.

Best wishes
Dylan

Deirdre McQuillan

Fashion Editor, *The Irish Times*, Dublin

Dear Molly

I have just realised to my shame that I never replied to your letter regarding your style bible book and your request for my favourite item of clothing. Please forgive me but September and October were very busy months that took in trips to Australia, London and Spain, while keeping up my regular columns and indeed looking after family responsibilities.

My favourite item of clothing, or one of them, is a long blue-black cable-knit cashmere coat by Lainey Keogh that has a special resonance as I bought it when we sold our house and moved to another one. It means something else as I am the author of a book on the history of the Aran sweater and feel that when you wear something that a pair of hands has knitted, you have a special connection with the maker.

Hope this is not too late and forgive me again for such a long delay in replying.

Every success in your effort to make a difference; I was in Ethiopia last year (both in Addis Ababa and Lalibela) and it is a unique and wonderful country.

Kind regards
Deirdre

Martin Mansergh

Politician, County Tipperary

Dear Molly

Thank you for your letter. I am not sure that I could be described as stylish but probably the most interesting part of my wardrobe is the tie drawer. There are some lovely silk ties, many of them Liberty, which I have been given as presents by wife and family.

Then there are ties of clubs and associations given on occasion of visits and speaking engagements, such as the centenary tie of Warrenpoint Golf Club, where my great-granduncle was secretary for about twenty years; a Harland and Wolff tie (the Belfast shipyard that built the *Titanic*), a couple of Ennis ties and so on.

Delegates to European Council meetings attended by EU heads of government were usually given ties marking those held under the presidency of a particular member state, so I have, for example, ties with EU stars from former French, German and Portuguese presidencies.

Now and again I buy art ties: for example, one depicting the spires of Spain's most extraordinary church, the Sagrada Familia, in Barcelona, or the famous Spanish painter Goya's portrait of King Charles III (1759-88) as an elderly man leaning on a hunting gun. I also have a number of green ties for wearing on St Patrick's Day.

I wish you all the best with your project.

With kind regards
Yours sincerely
Martin Mansergh

Eve Murray

Human Resources, Harvey Nichols, Dublin

Dear Molly

Thank you so much for your letter. Please excuse my slow response: as you may know we have just held our annual autumn-winter fashion show. This is a very interesting project and for a great cause. We wish you the best of luck with it and look forward to seeing the finished product.

As for the most stylish thing in my wardrobe, it's difficult to pinpoint. I am a big believer in the little black dress. I wear some variation on the LBD every day. I love 1950s style clothing and prom dresses in particular. The silhouette suits all body types.

Dresses can be a little sedate and especially as I wear a lot of black dresses, can become a little repetitive. It is for this reason that I have to say that the stylish stars of my wardrobe would be the shoes that complete an outfit.

I often pair an unexpected footwear choice with a pretty dress to 'toughen it up a bit'. I love to wear a pretty 1950s silhouette with big clunky studded boots by Jeffrey Campbell and a cropped leather biker jacket. I love the dramatic styles from Jeffrey Campbell which add theatre to an outfit (without having to be brave with statement clothing pieces).

Shoes are my favourite things to buy as I can keep them for years and not grow out of them. Of all my shoes, these are currently my absolute favourite and in my opinion the most stylish item in my wardrobe.

Kind regards
Eve Murray

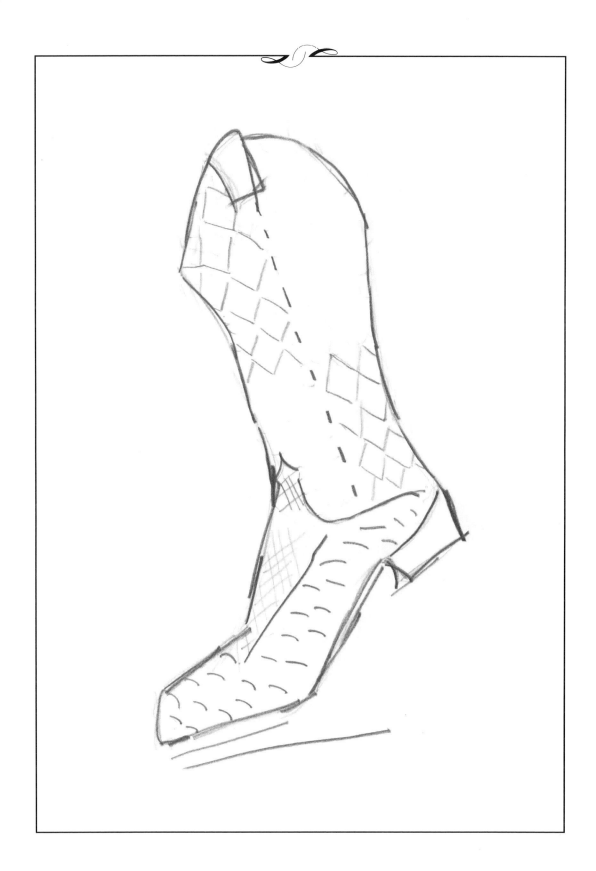

David Norris

Senator, Dublin

Dear Molly

Thank you very much indeed for your kind letter, which I was delighted to receive. It is most generous and thoughtful of you to raise funds for orphan children in Ethiopia and Kenya and in such an unique way. May I say first of all that your surname is most unusual and the only other Parmeter that I am aware of is a man by the name of Louis Parmeter who is involved in St Patrick's Cathedral. It is nice to hear of another.

Regarding my most stylish item, that would have to be a pair of handmade boots I purchased in Austin, Texas, many years ago. When visiting that great city of Austin, I popped into a store to get some cold remedies and across the road from the store I spotted a shop called The Boot and Saddle. I crossed over and discovered that it was run by a man over a hundred years of age and his trusty little dog. We had a long and enjoyable chat. He explained that the shop specialised in selling handmade cowboy boots that retailed at approximately $1000-$1500. Naturally the cost was beyond my budget but seeing my interest he kindly offered to let me purchase a pair of handmade snakeskin boots which somebody had almost completely paid for, bar an outstanding $65, almost five years previously, and assuming that they were now not going to complete the purchase he offered them to me! I was absolutely thrilled! And in fact I wore them recently to the *VIP* Style Awards!

I hope you enjoy the story.

With very best wishes to you and your charitable efforts. You are a credit to both your family and your school.

Yours sincerely
David Norris

Kate O'Dwyer

Kalu Boutique, Naas, County Kildare

Dear Molly

Thank you so much for including me in your style bible. You are an amazing, inspirational girl and I am sure you must be one of a kind.

My special piece in my wardrobe is my Maria Grachvogel black lace dress, a beautiful timeless piece which I will wear forever.

Let me know if you need any further information, I would love to see the book once published. I am sure it will be fabulous.

Warm regards
Kate
xx

PS Apologies for the delay in replying

Aedeen O'Hagan

Director, Aedeen O'Hagan School of Ballet, Carlow

Dear Molly

You are a busy young lady and your book sounds like a super idea.

My most stylish piece of clothing is a leather jacket! It just about covers my hips, it's soft pink leather, no collar, three-quarter-length sleeves, two neat pockets, hook-and-eye fasteners and floral lining.

It comes out of the wardrobe every now and then and I hope it will be 'timeless'.

Good luck with your book.

All the best
Aedeen

Bronagh O'Sullivan

Bow and Pearl Boutique, Ranelagh, Dublin

Hi Molly

The most stylish piece in my wardrobe is a vintage statement necklace. I wear it with almost everything, from a dressy dress to a simple T-shirt.

Best of luck with your book.

Bronagh

Patrick Plunkett

Professor of Emergency Medicine, St James's Hospital

Dear Molly

Please accept my apologies for the delay in replying to your letter about style icons.

I am delighted (but a bit embarrassed!) to be considered a 'style icon'.

The most stylish item in my wardrobe is, I think, my collection of ties. For the past thirty years, I have worn only bow ties. These tend to be more flamboyant than 'long ties' and are evocative of a stylish past, principally Edwardian.

When I was a young doctor, I found that the starch from latex gloves ruined my long ties, as I had to keep tucking them into my shirt. A bow tie eliminates the problem of a tie dangling as I lean over a patient.

In the NHS (next island to the east), ties are no longer allowed as they are considered fomites (look it up). Bow ties are, however, acceptable, so my ties are not only fashionable but practical.

Your fundraising idea is a wonderful one and I hope you manage to send more money to educate those less fortunate than you.

Le gach dea-ghuí
Is mise
Patrick Plunkett

PS Example of my item enclosed.

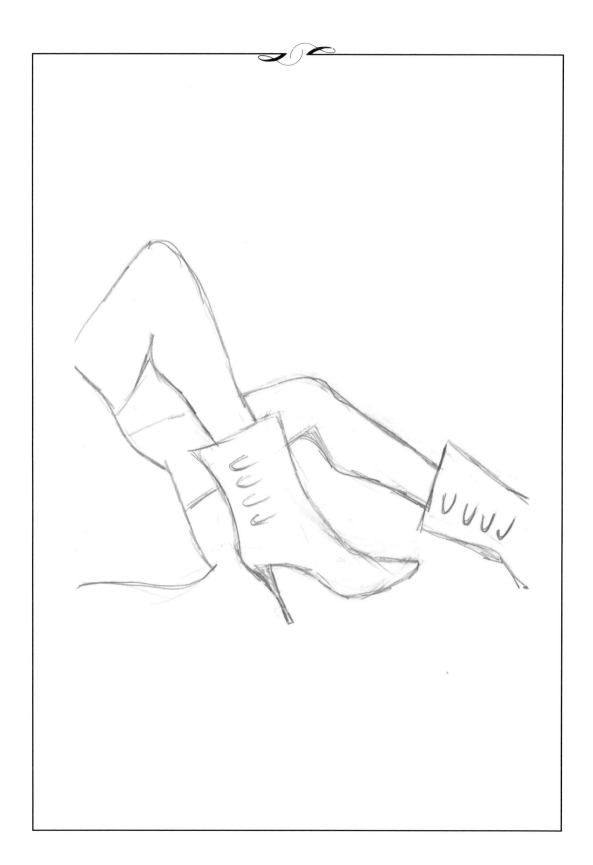

Terry Prone

Communications Consultant, Dublin

Dear Molly

I should apologise that it's taken me so long to respond to your letter but I won't. The reason for the delay was that I kept rereading it every day for the sheer pleasure of going through something so clear, so charming, so informative and so flattering.

I'm a big fan of charity shops – and a regular customer – so if I can help, I'd be delighted to do so.

My style icon item is a pair of boots with safety pins going up the side. I can take a picture and send it to you. Or, if boots don't do it for you, let me know and I'll think of something else.

Yours sincerely
Terry Prone

Feargal Quinn

Senator, Dublin

Dear Molly

Many thanks for your very interesting letter – I enjoyed it hugely.

Molly, I've been called many things in my life…but it's the first time ever that someone referred to me as a 'style icon'! I can't wait to see what you do with your life! Politics maybe? Whatever it is, I know you will be most successful.

Men don't have the same opportunities as women to be stylish or to show their personality in their clothes. In my case, I tend to make my statement with very colourful ties and equally colourful socks. I have found that people will remember my socks or ties but may not remember what I am saying!

I wish you every success with your project and with your book. I look forward to having a copy of it.

With best wishes
Senator Feargal Quinn

Dickie Rock

Singer, Dublin

Dear Molly

I am sorry for the delay in answering your letter and I am flattered that you describe me as a 'style icon'.

I suppose as I am a singer/entertainer, the clothes I wear on stage would be my most stylish.

At the moment my choice for stage is a black suit, white shirt and black tie, loosely knotted (so I can breathe more easily).

I also have a grey-blue suit I wear with a pale pink shirt and without a tie, depending on the venue. Also clean black shoes.

I hope this will be of some help to you. Of course, when not on stage I like smart casual clothes.

If you need any more information, call me.

Dickie Rock

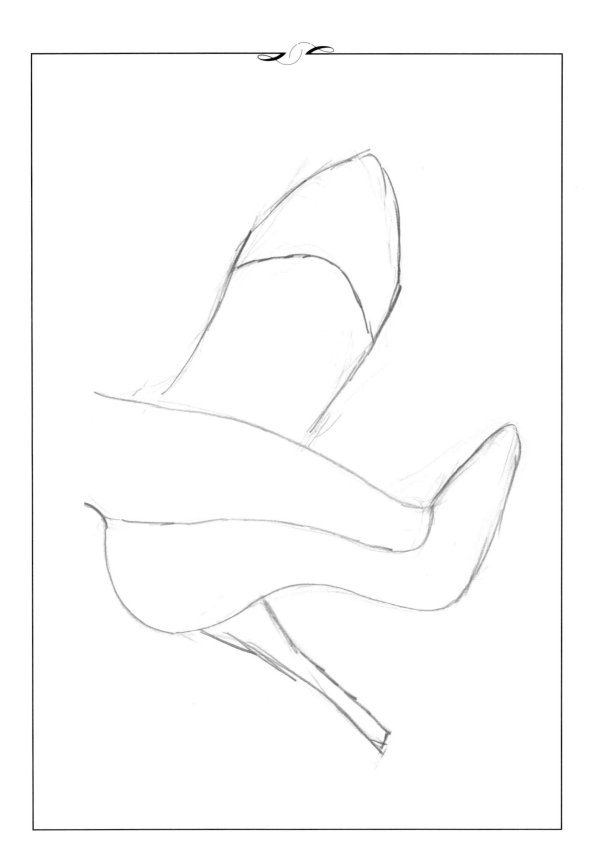

Danielle Ryan

Actress and Philanthropist

Dearest Molly

Sincere apologies for the delay in responding to your beautiful letter. I must admit that I was extremely flattered that you would consider including me in your style bible. It is a wonderful idea and very clever of you to come up with such an interesting concept to raise money for the children in Ethiopia and Kenya. You may be aware of the philanthropic work that my family and I have been involved with over the past number of years. We have completed two very different projects to date with the opening of the Lir Academy in Dublin and also our work with UNICEF Ireland in Sri Lanka. I know that it is extremely rewarding to help people in need but it can sometimes be a difficult job to encourage others to champion your cause and get assistance and support to the people who really need it. You should be very proud of yourself for undertaking such a commitment, especially at your age.

Now, to answer your question: what is my favourite item of clothing? My favourite item of clothing is actually a pair of black Manolo Blahnik shoes. I love these shoes because they are very classy, which means I can wear them for business meetings and with a dress to dinner. I can also wear them with jeans and a nice fitted blazer, so they are very versatile. I think they can make any outfit look chic and, as such, they are a staple of my wardrobe.

I hope this helps with your charity project, Molly. You might send me the details of the charity shop in Carlow that you are hoping to assist, as I would really like to send them a small donation, to get things started for you. In the meantime if you have any further questions for the style bible, please do not hesitate to get in touch with my office by phone. Best of luck with it all.

Yours sincerely
Danielle Ryan

Karl Patrick Smith

Stylist, Dublin

Hi Molly

Hope you are keeping very well!

Many apologies for my late reply. I have had a very busy few weeks but I was delighted to read your letter and I'm very flattered you thought of me to include in this project. I am very impressed at your idea of the style bible, I really think this is a wonderful, innovative way to help the children of Ethiopia and Kenya, so well done!

As regards the stylish item you requested, I would have to say that in my opinion, a fitted blazer is a piece that every woman should have in their wardrobe. It should have a few details to keep it as a timeless piece for many years. It should be black, fitted at the waist, with a narrow lapel, should end just below the hip, have a vent from below the waist on the back and have no more than two buttons. A blazer can be worn over a T-shirt or blouse, paired with jeans during the day, with a skirt or trousers for work, or over a nice silk dress at night-time.

I hope this will help in some way towards your book and if you need anything else please do contact me again.

Also, I have a few little bits that I would like to send you. I am working this week but will hopefully get them in the post to you by the end of this week!

Thanks again for your letter, I really appreciate it very much!

Karl Patrick

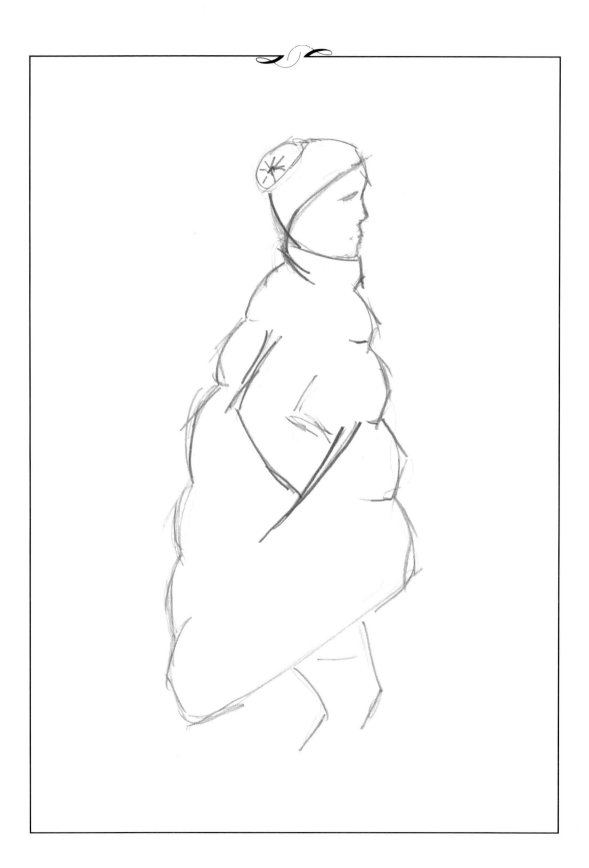

Helen Steele

Fashion Designer, Monaghan

Dear Molly

Thank you so much for writing to me. Sounds like you lead a really busy life, good for you. I must say I am really impressed by your letter.

I have enclosed my autumn-winter lookbook and have put an * beside all of the looks that I believe are very stylish. The must have for my wardrobe is the following:

A black Silver Hill duck-down puffa. (The 100% pure Irish down comes from my husband's ducks. I live on a farm in County Monaghan, which is pretty far from the catwalks and showrooms of London and Paris fashion weeks, where our autumn-winter 2012 and spring-summer 2013 collections have shown.) The puffa has a concealed hood that is very important if you live in Ireland – as you know, it rains loads!

So Molly if you have any other questions you can email me. I have also included a gift for you of a T-shirt from our spring-summer collection for 2013. I hope you like it. It is a print of local flowers in bloom.

Wishing you lots of luck. You deserve it. And keep up the hard work. It will pay off. Best of luck with fashion and art.

I will be reading about you, no doubt, in years to come!

Kindest regards
Helen Steele

Jennifer Stevens

Editor, *U Magazine*

Hi Molly

Sorry it has taken so long to get back to you – I just found your letter today.

My favourite item in my wardrobe is my Chanel 2.55 bag. It's a design classic and I had wanted one ever since I began working in the magazine industry. I made a big deal of buying it and met my best friend in London. We had an amazing day that culminated in a visit to the Chanel boutique on the Brompton Road. I made a beeline for the bag and handed over my hard-earned money. I love it as much today as the day I bought it seven years ago. I wear it casually with jeans to go shopping, or bring it with me to glamorous events.

It was so much money to spend but I know I will have it forever and pass it down in years to come.

I hope that's OK for you, Molly.

Best of luck with your project; it sounds brilliant.

Jennifer

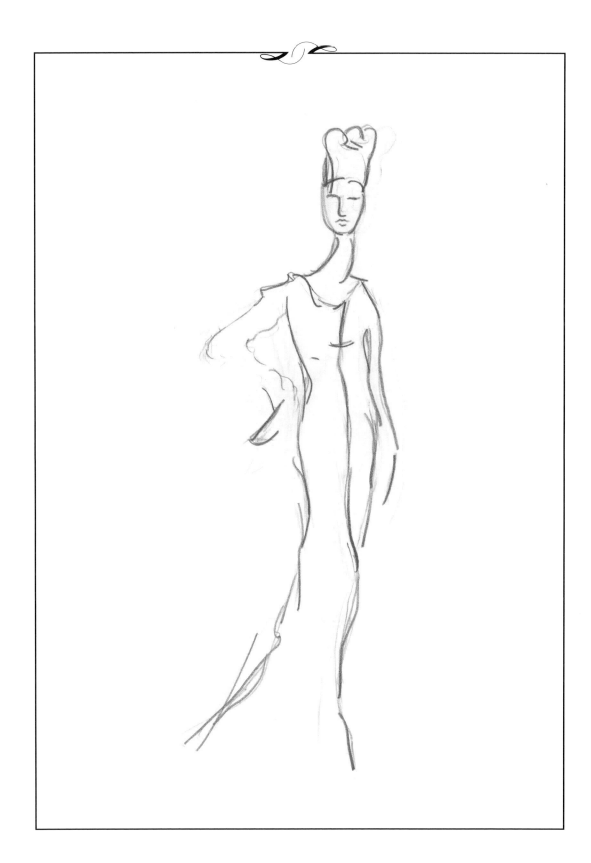

Kathryn Thomas

Broadcaster, Carlow

Dear Molly

Thanks so much for your letter. It sounds like a fabulous project and one I wish I had thought of when I was at school. I had heard of Chic and Cheerful and glad to hear the shop is going well. I've been to Ethiopia and I loved every minute of it. The people are so lovely, although very poor in some parts – so your mum is doing great work.

My most stylish item in my wardrobe is a full-length gold evening dress by Temperley. It is covered with fine lace and I bought it years ago and have worn it to five different events. If I'm photographed in it, I have to wait another year before I can wear it again!

Good luck with your style bible and with everything you do.

Sending you big hugs
Kathryn Thomas

J.P. McManus

Horse Breeder and Businessman, County Limerick

Dear Molly

Your recent letter addressed to J.P. McManus has been referred to the board of the J.P. McManus Charitable Foundation for attention.

The board notes your plan to create a style bible this year in circumstances where any sale proceeds may be applied in support of the charitable activities of Chic and Cheerful in Ethiopia and Kenya.

As a result of your request, the board has made an award in the sum of €1000 in support of the activities of Love Shack Kenya and a cheque for this amount is enclosed for application on this basis.

Yours sincerely
P. Gerard Boland

and finally...

"

Fashion is a form of ugliness so intolerable that we have
to alter it every six months.

"

Oscar Wilde

Fashion changes but style endures.

Coco Chanel